ZAPEDELIC #2

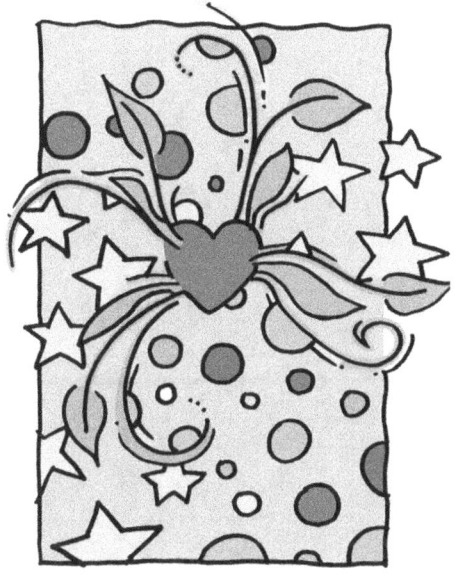

COLORING BOOK

15
READY-TO-COLOR
PSYCHEDELIC
DRAWINGS!

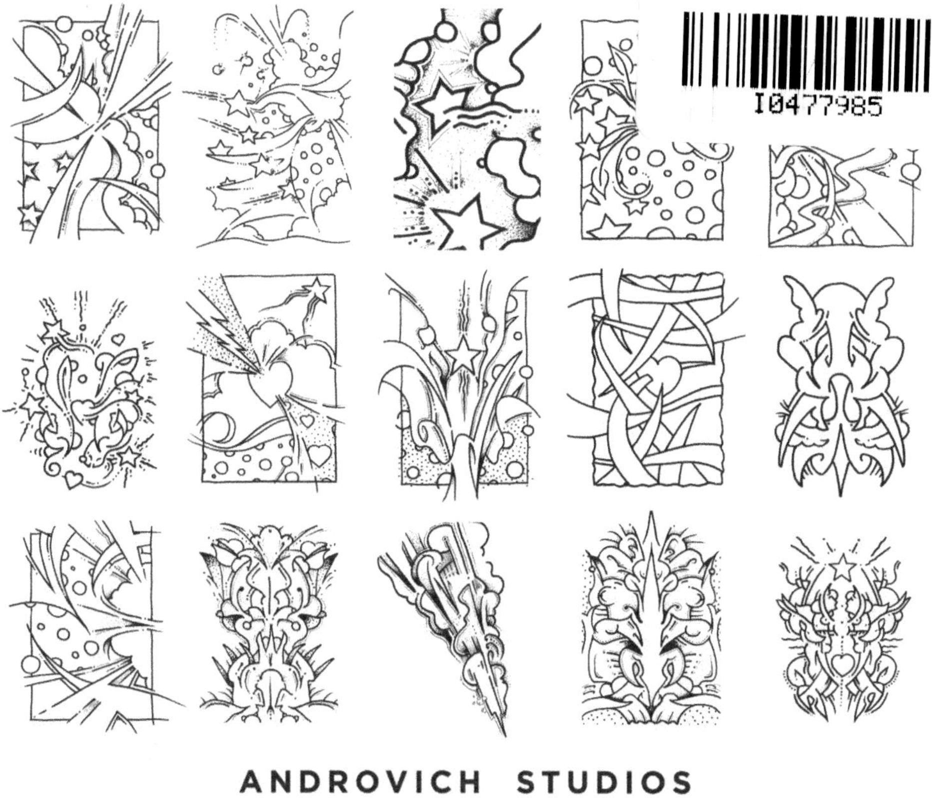

ANDROVICH STUDIOS

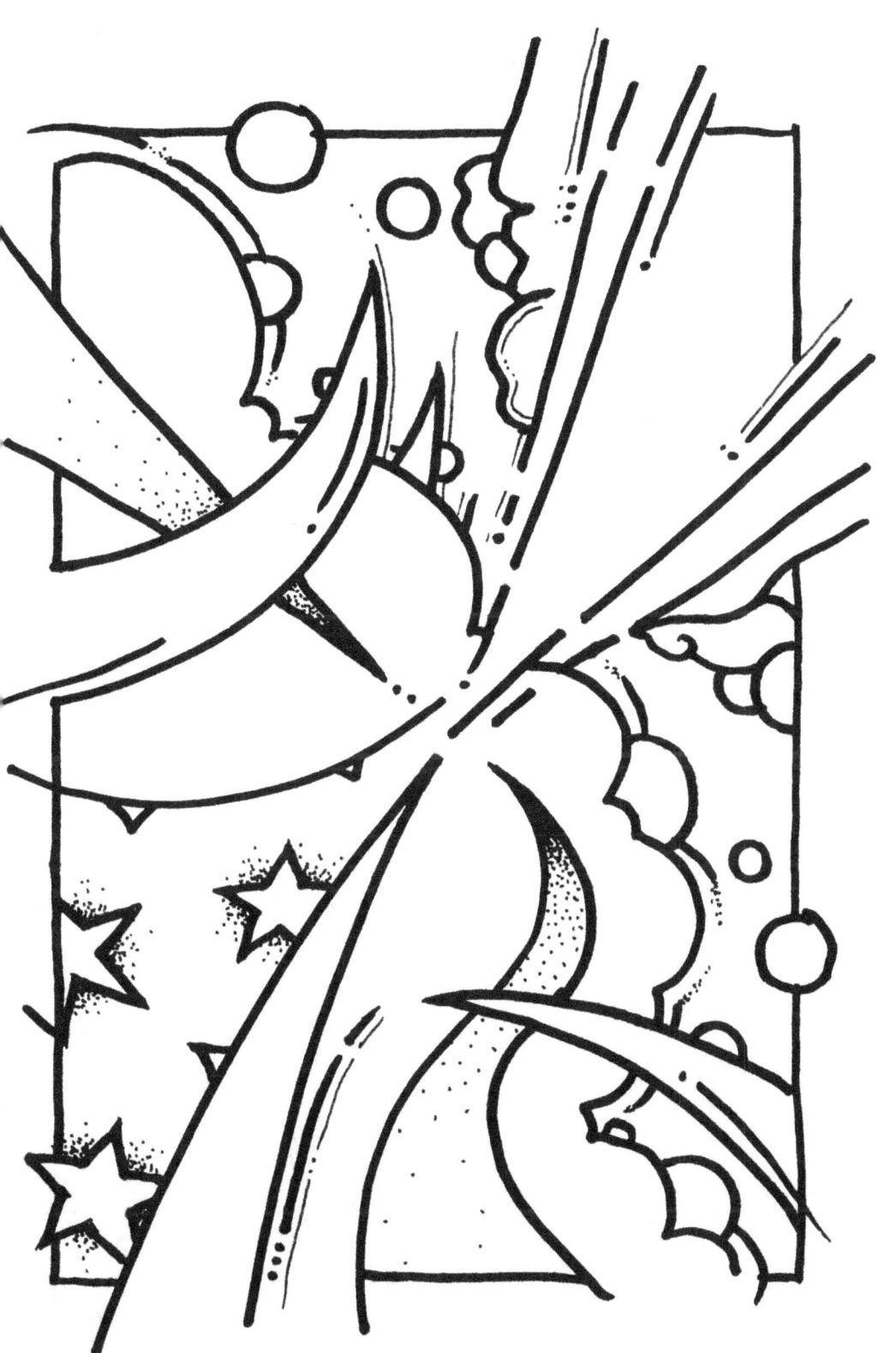

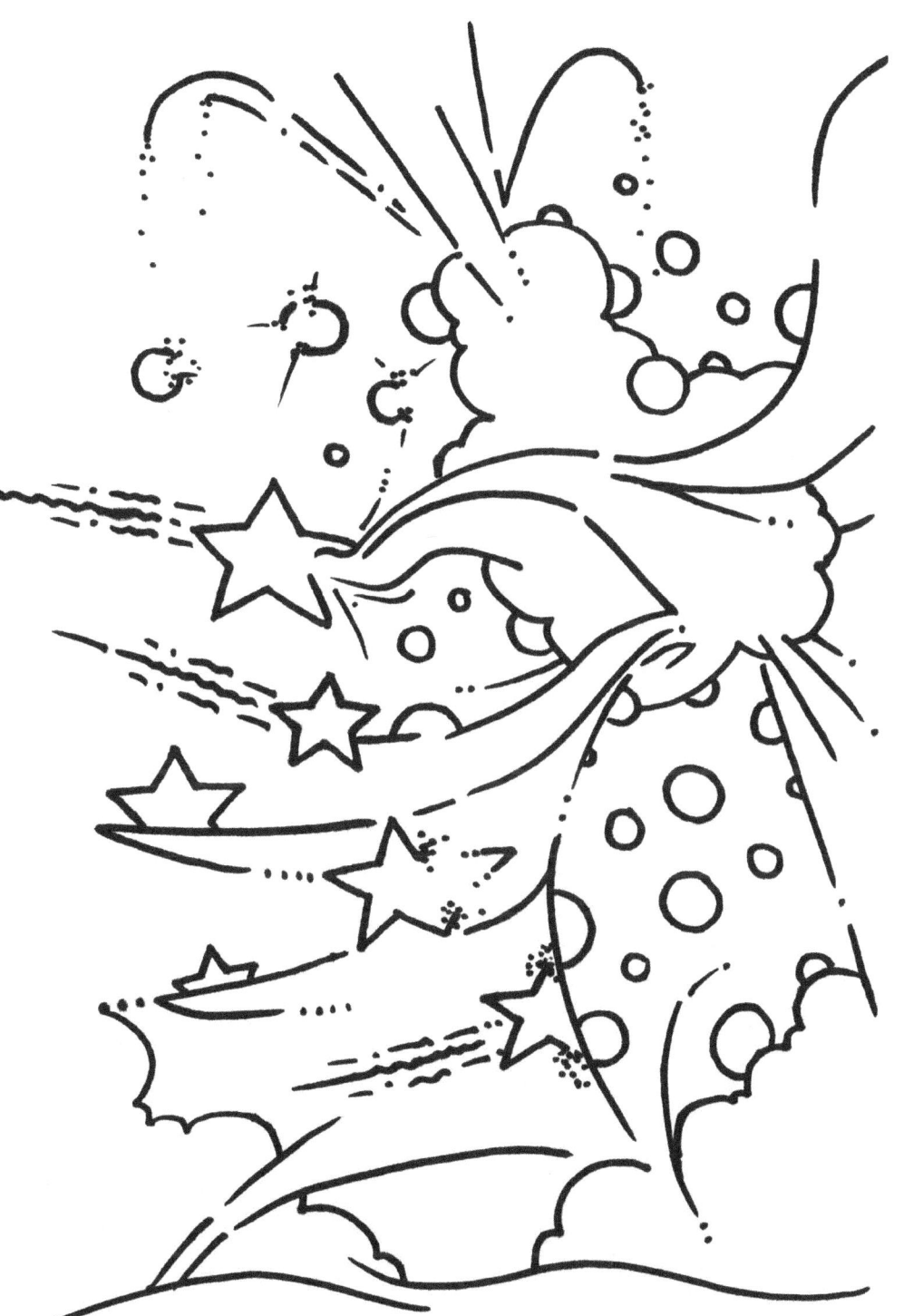

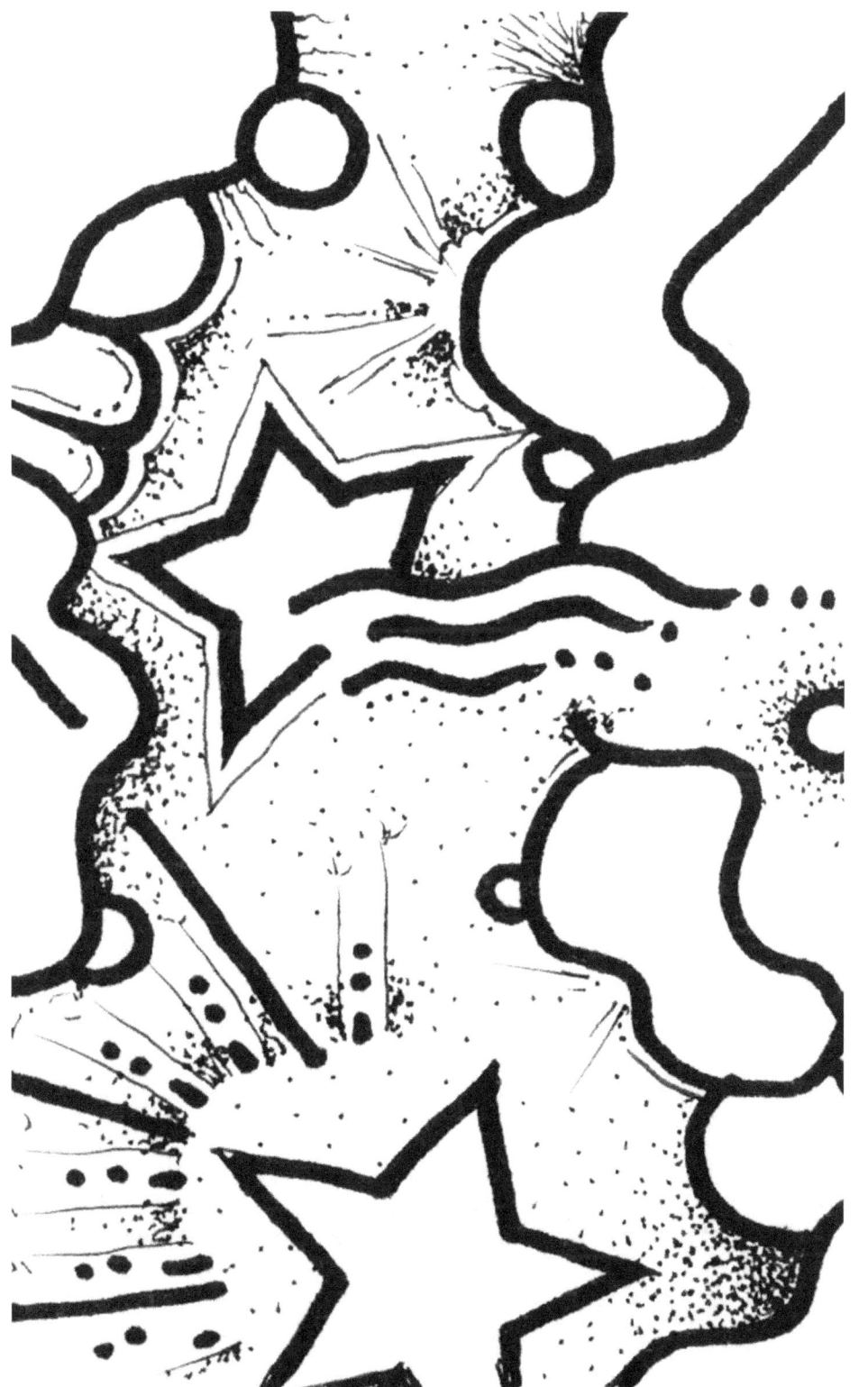

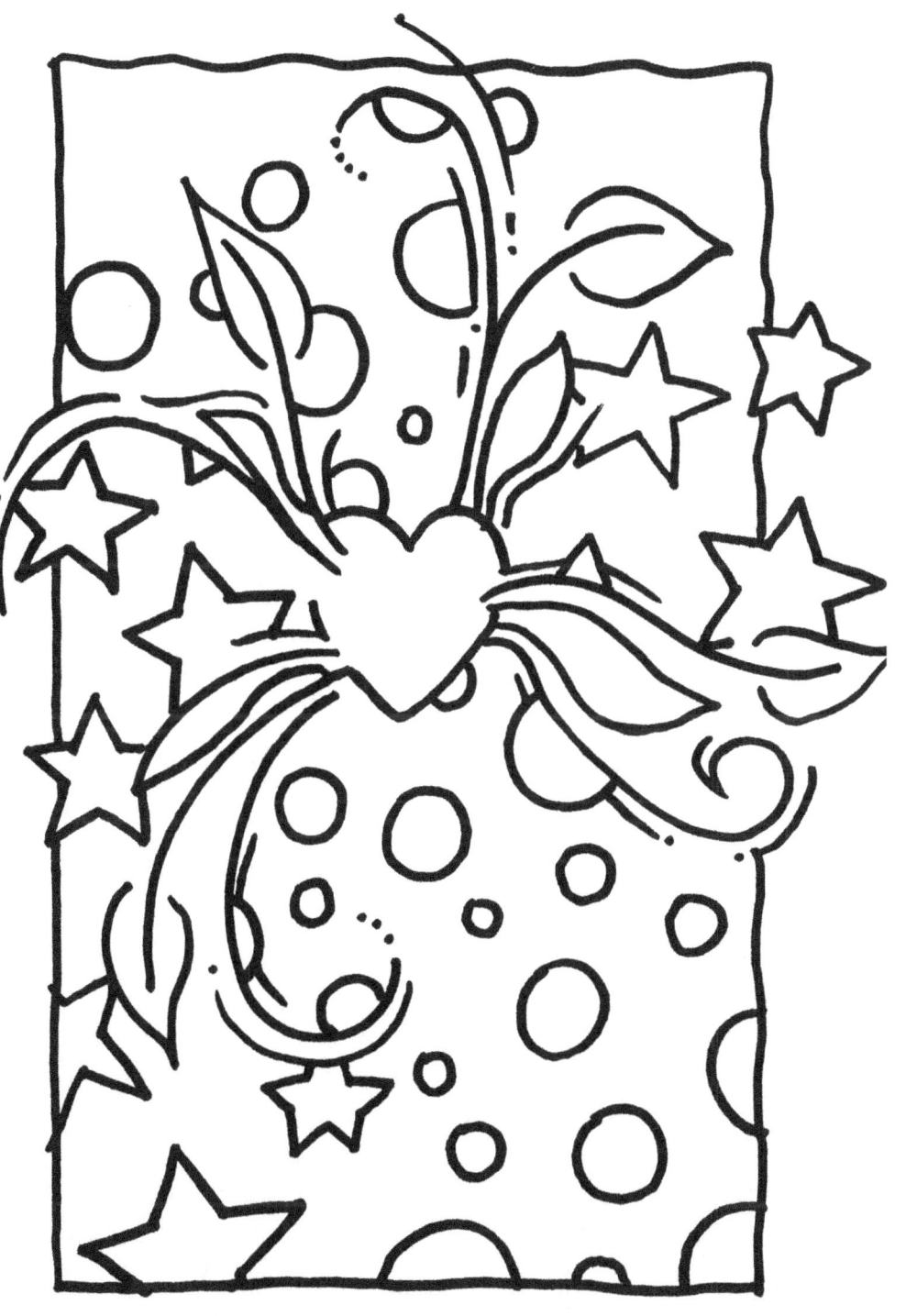

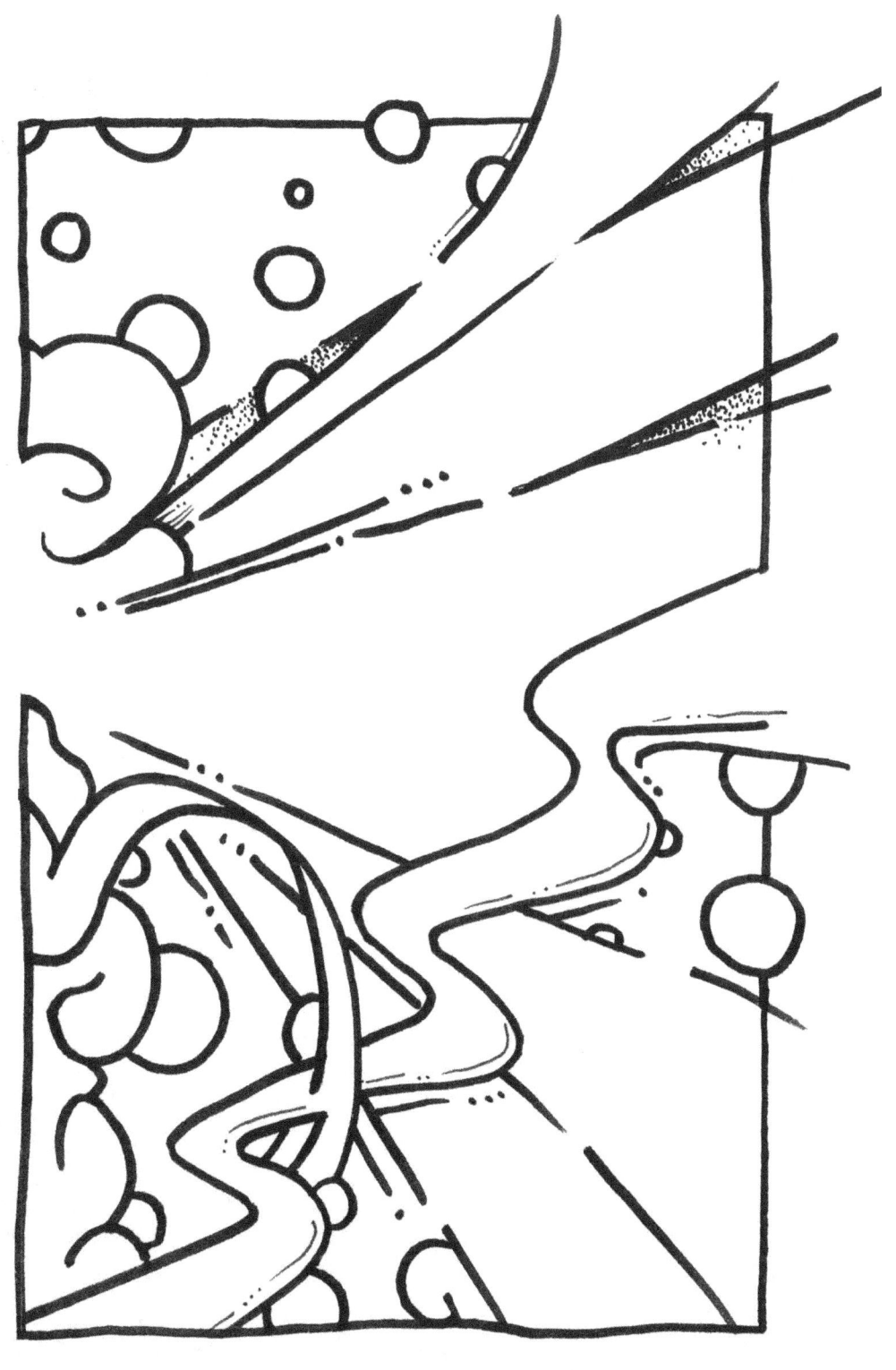

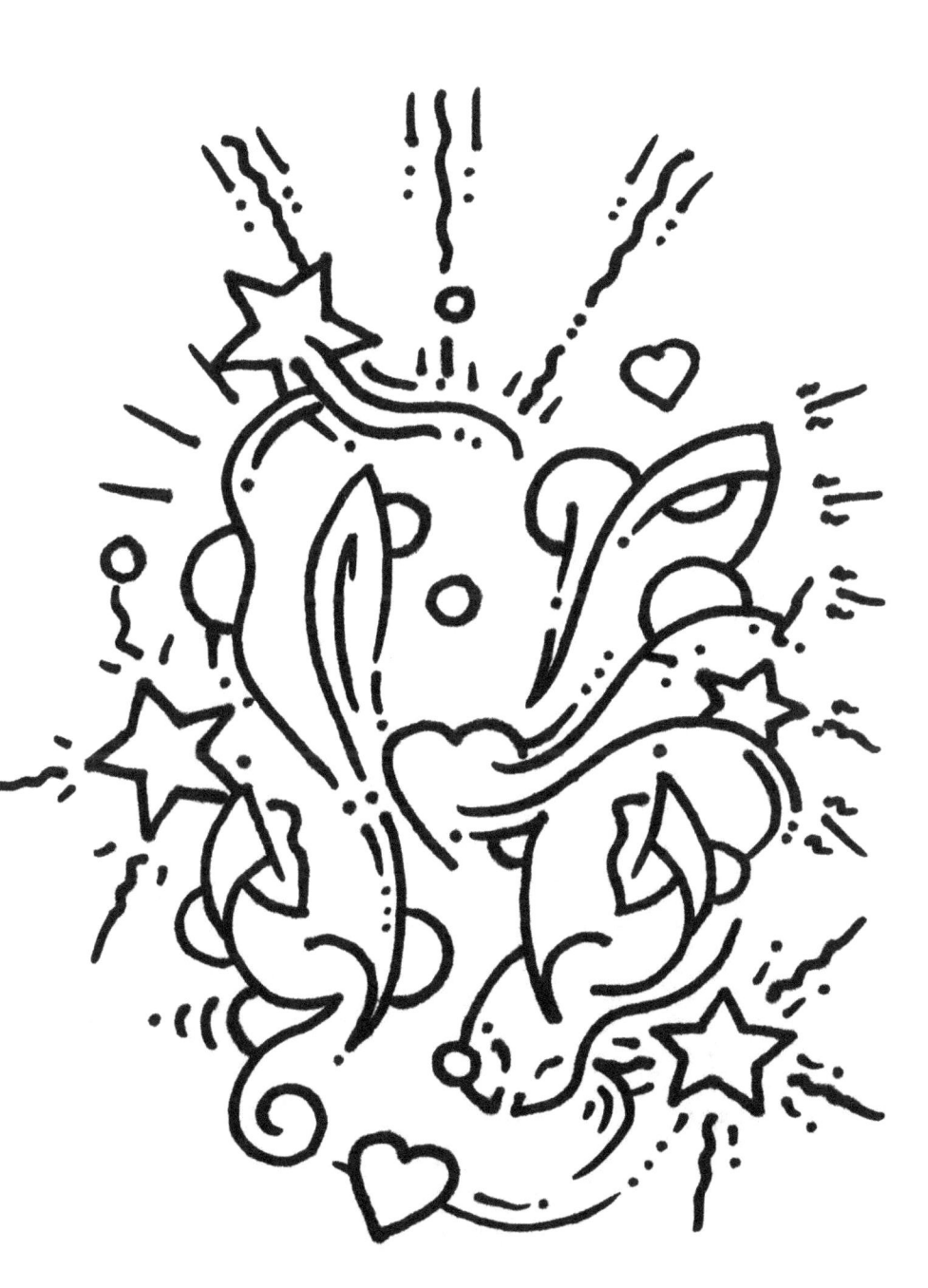

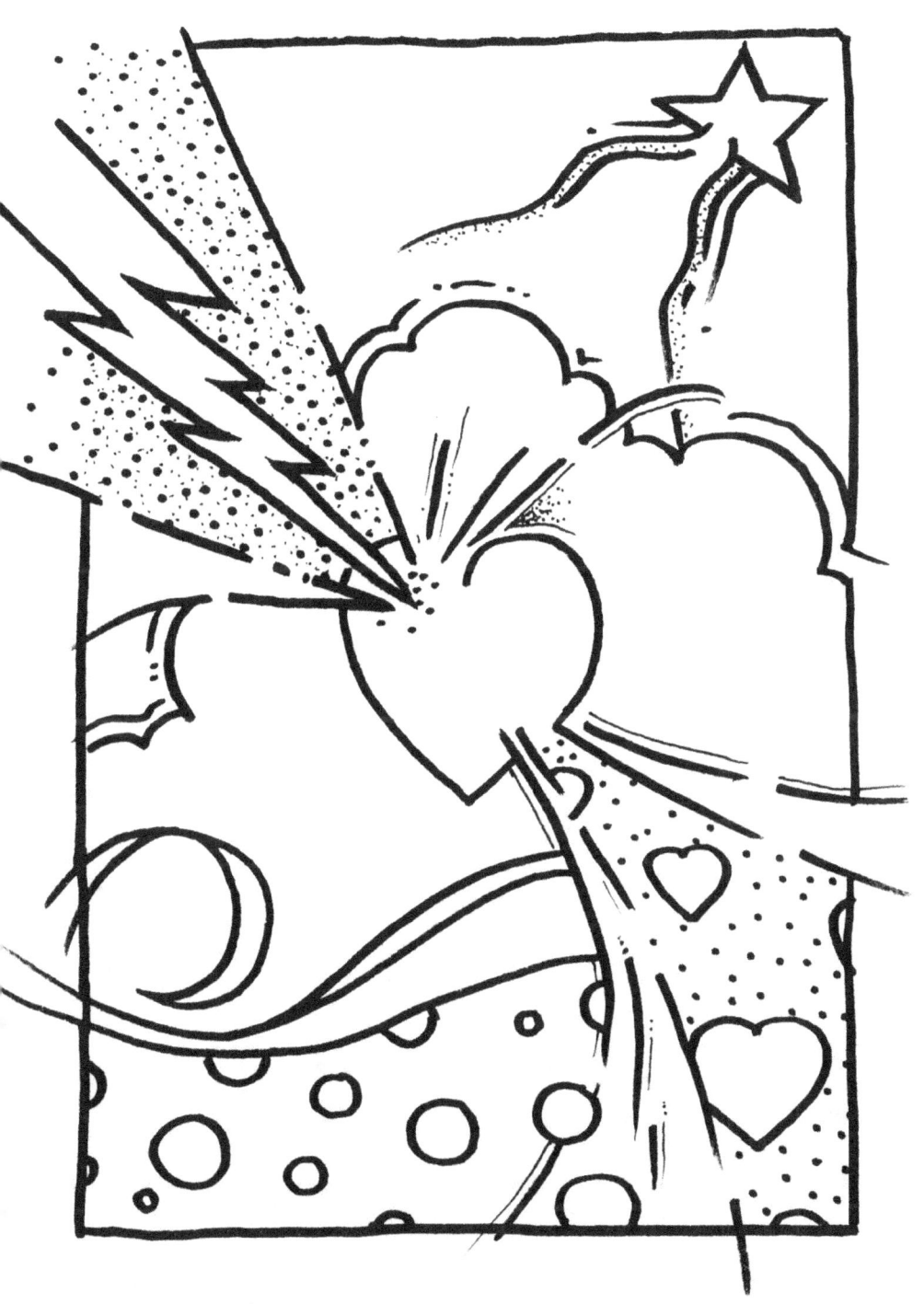

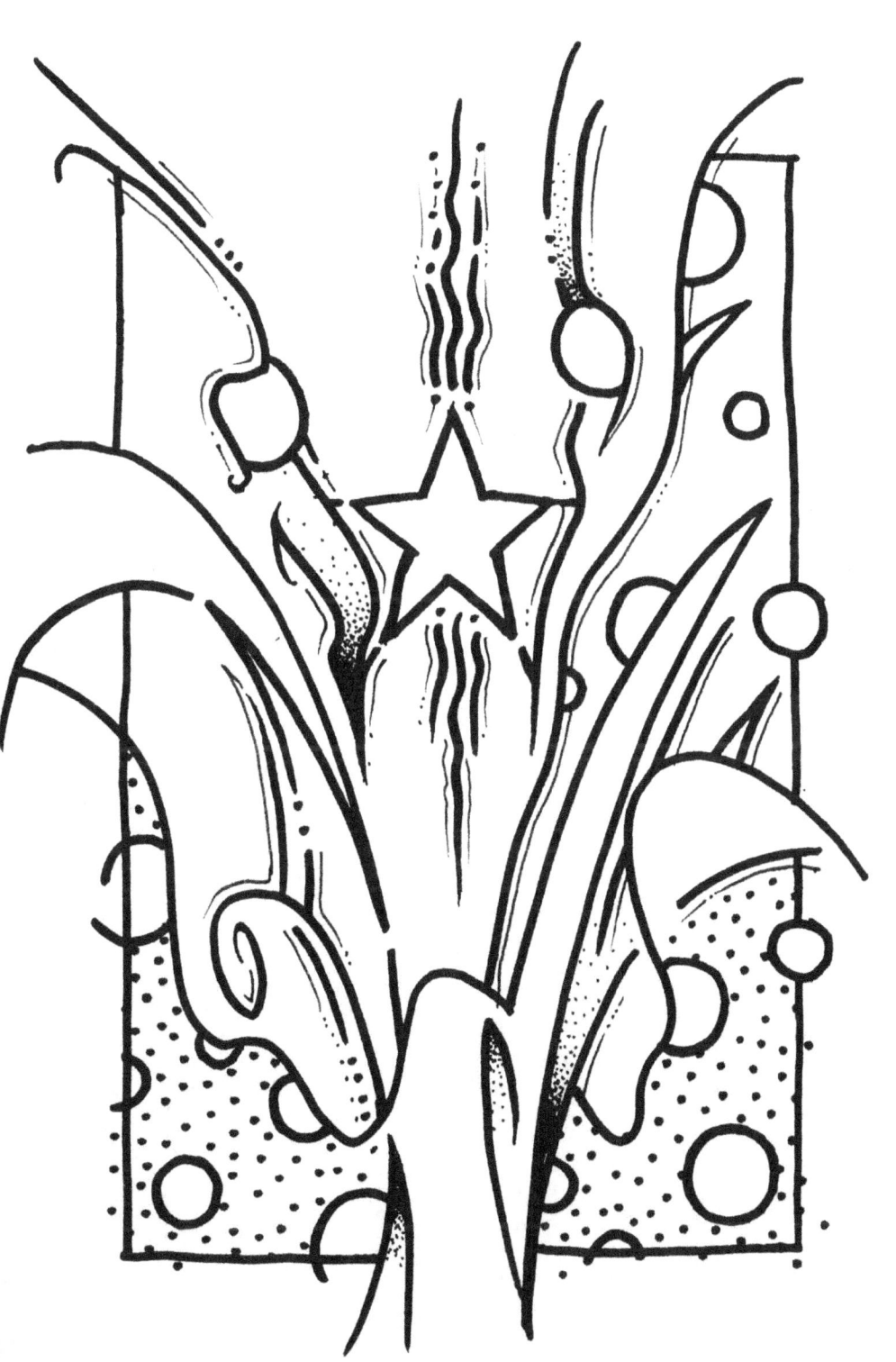

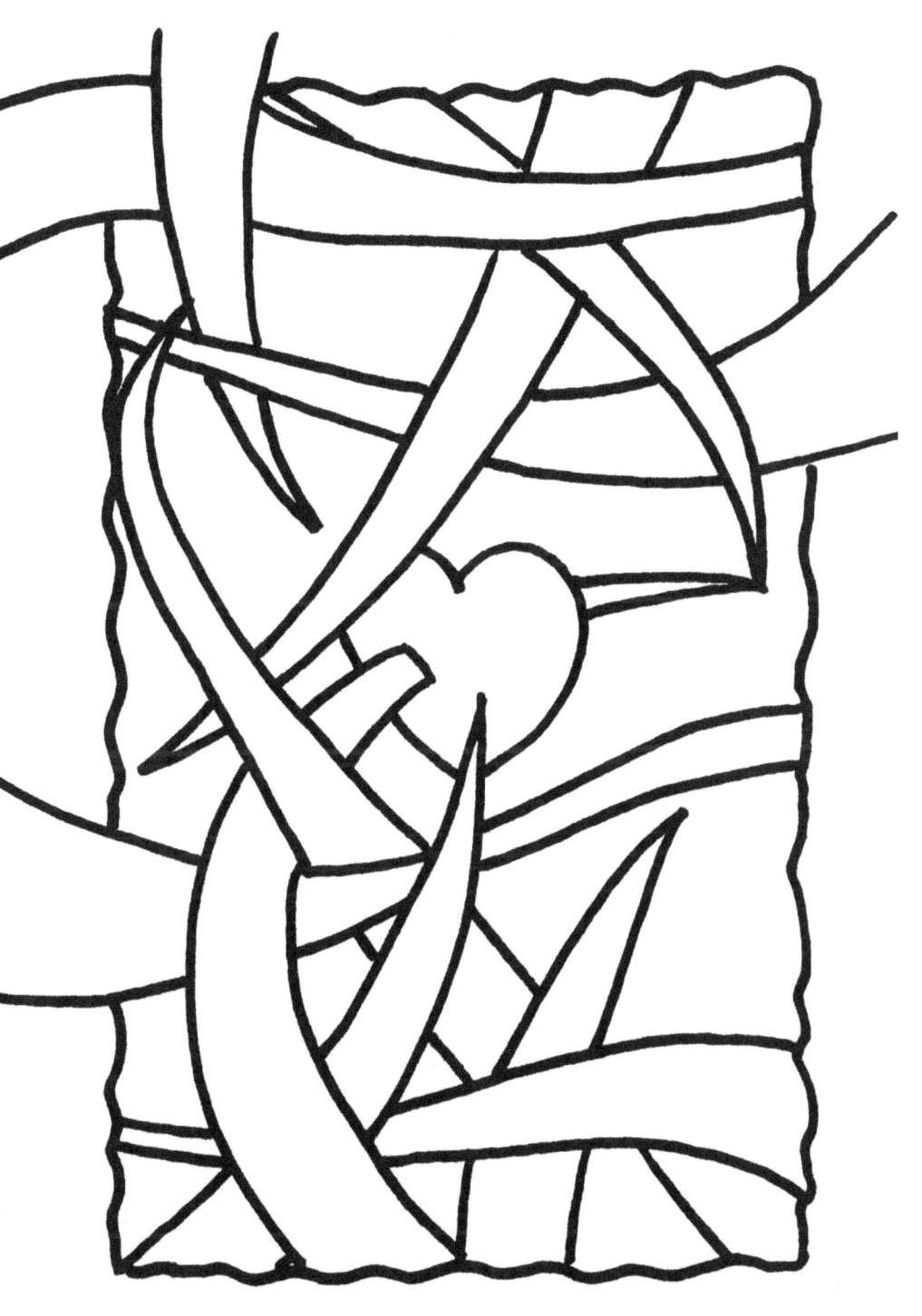

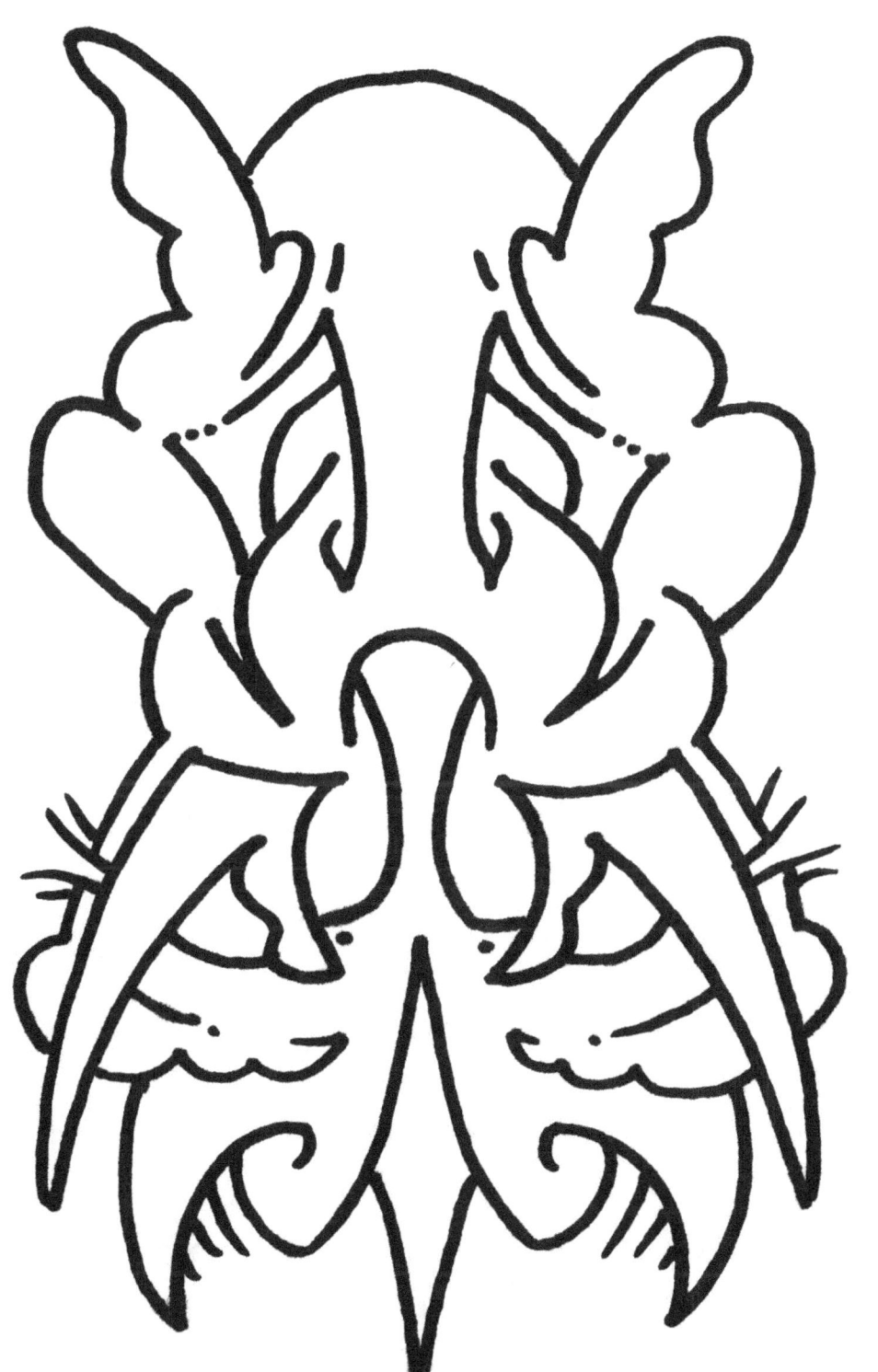

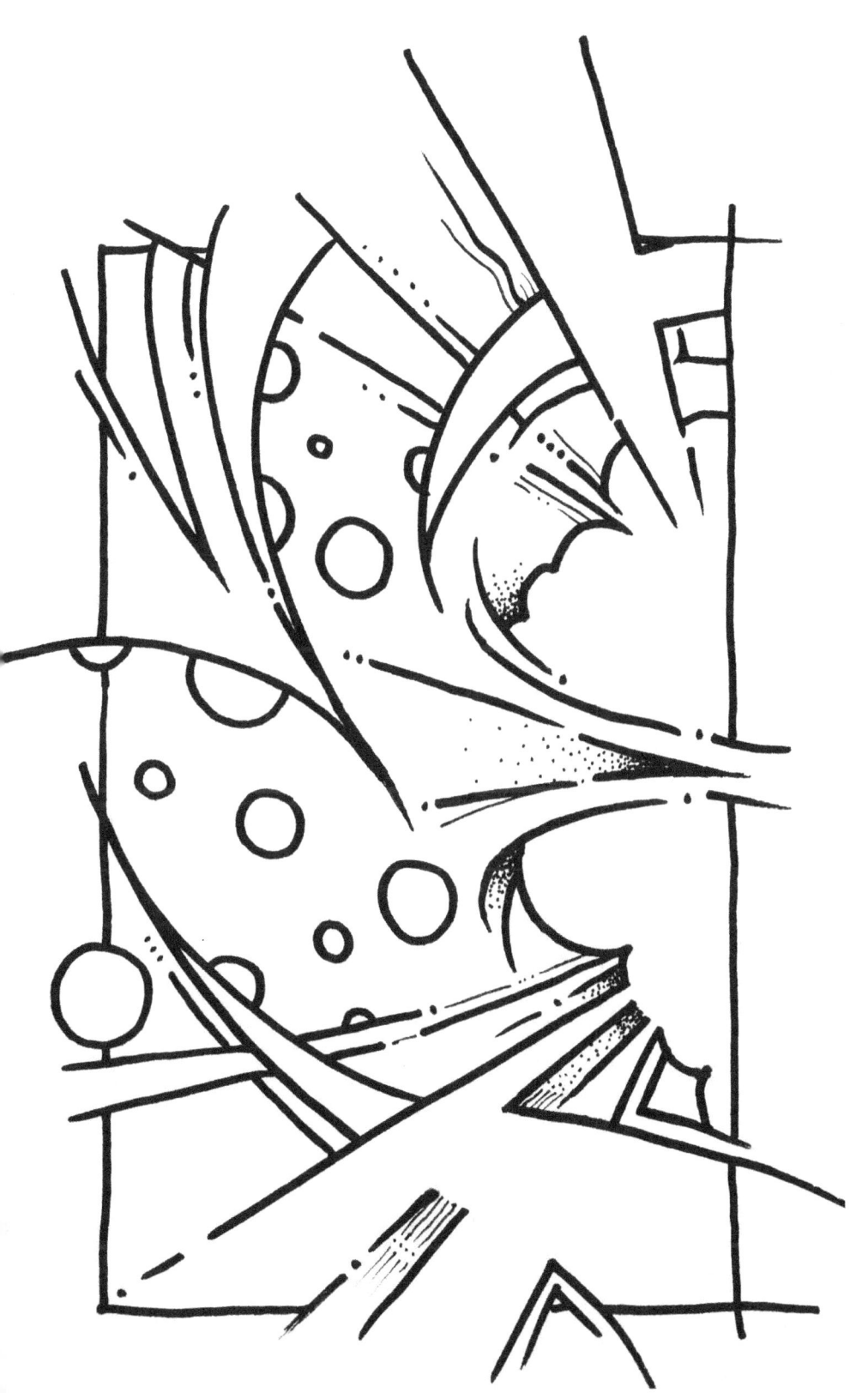

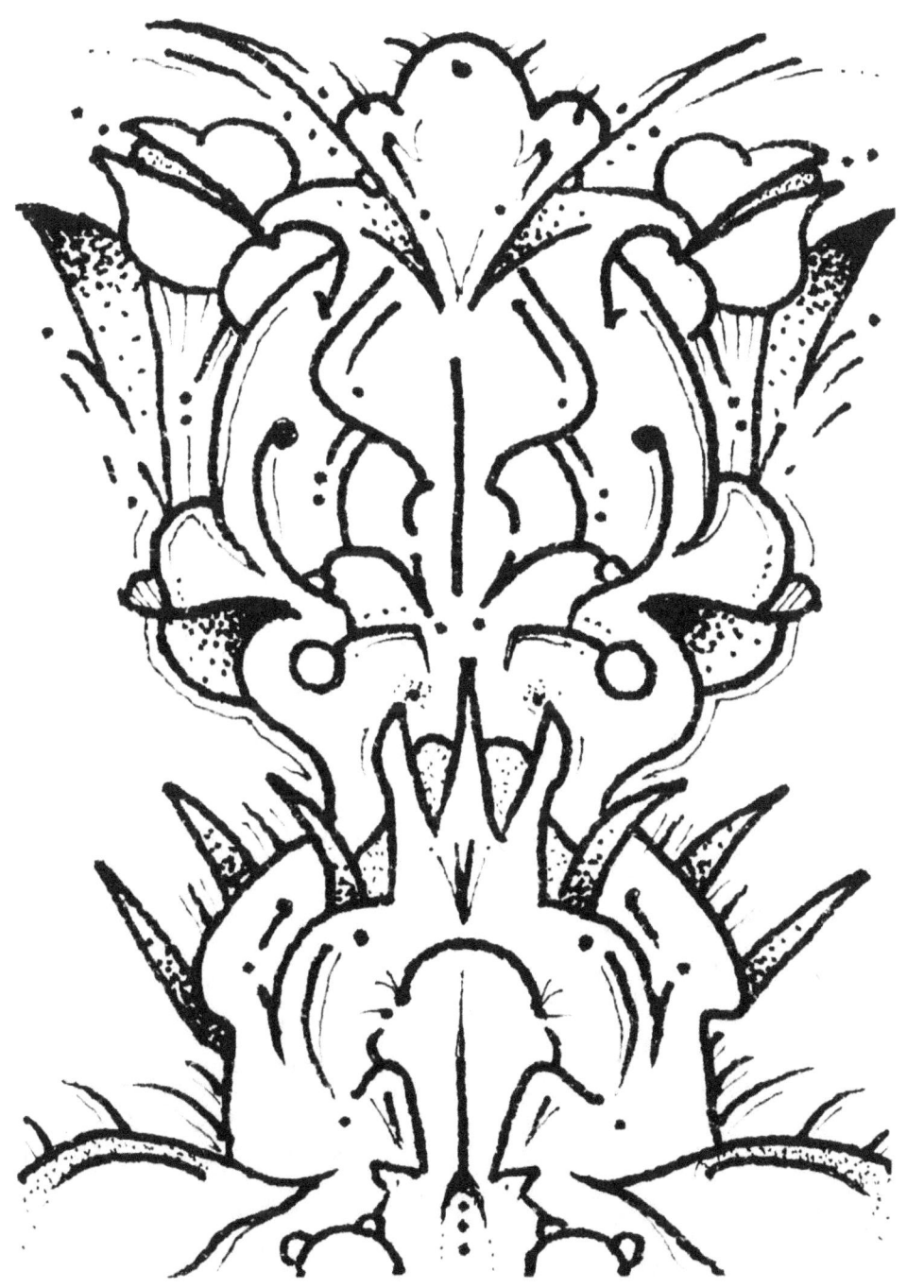

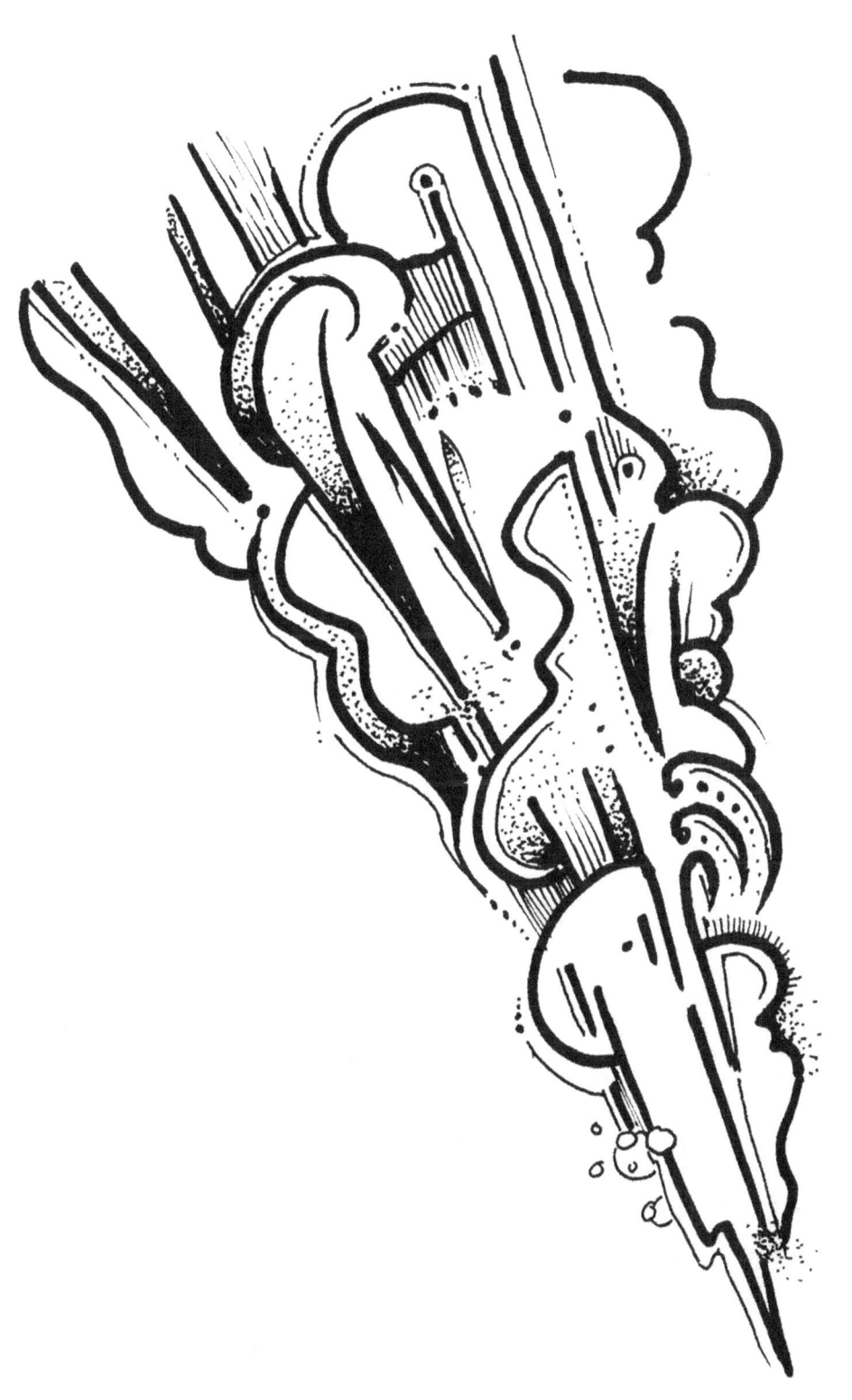

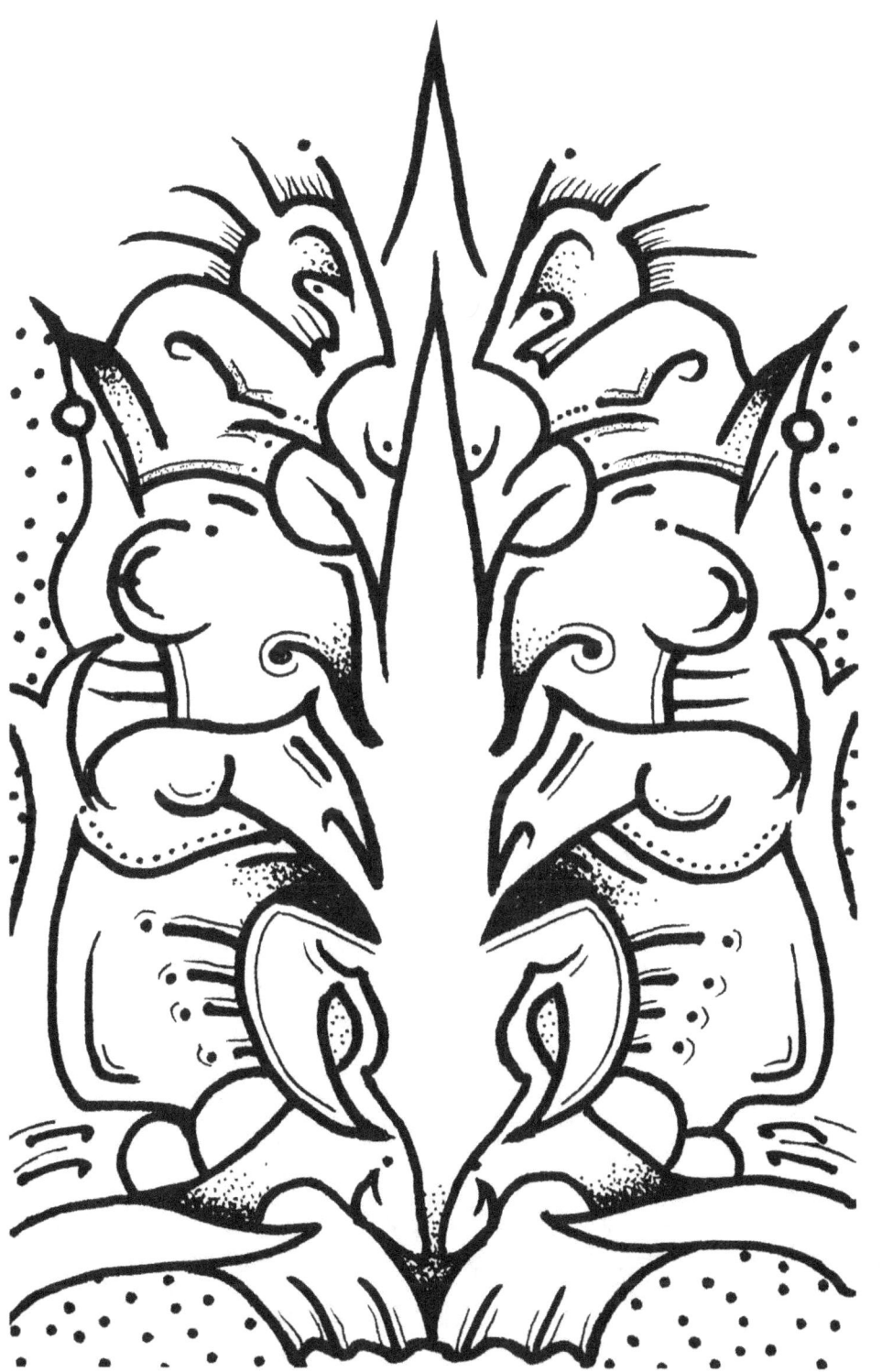

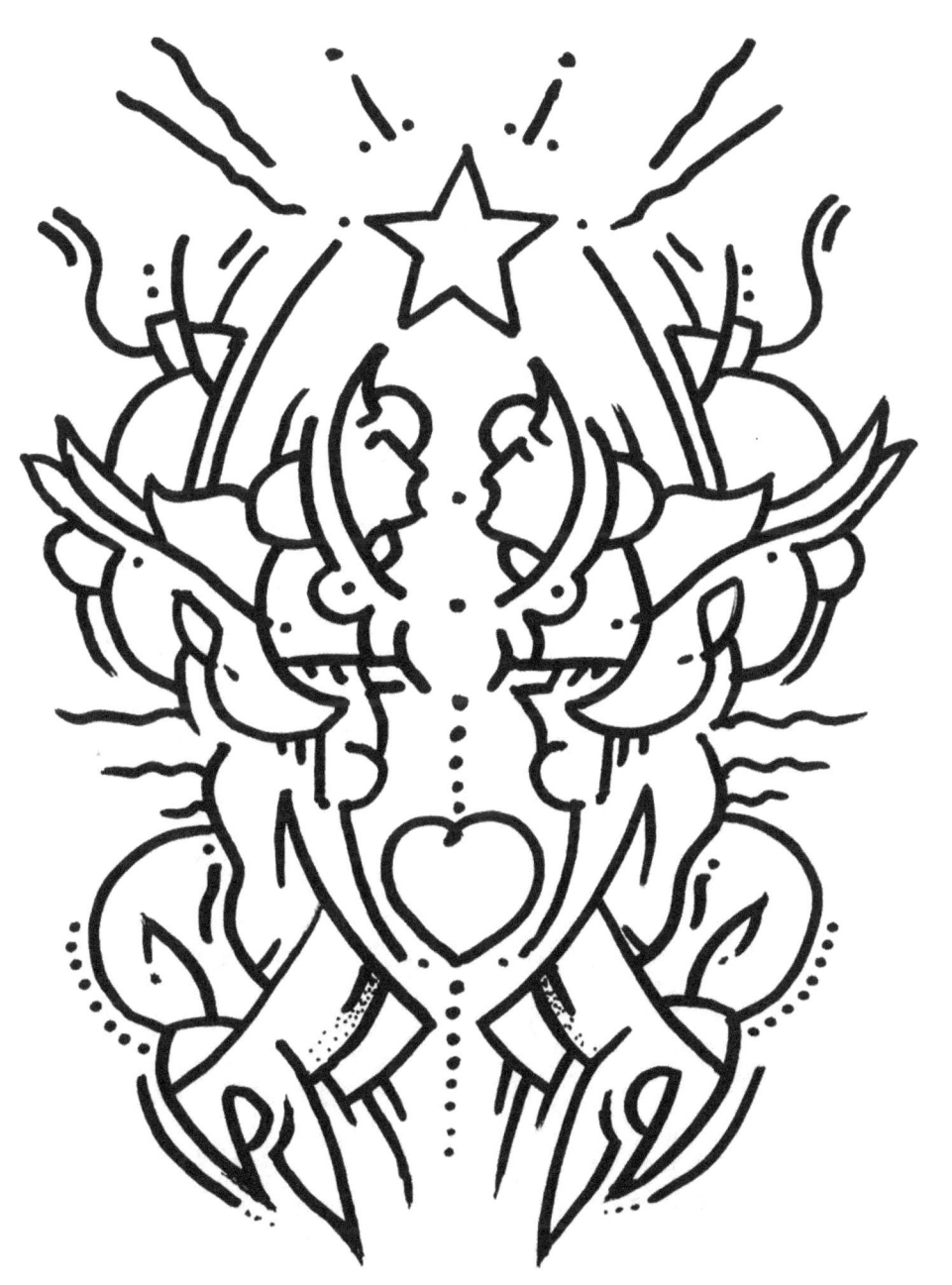

www.ingramcontent.com/pod-product-compliance
Lightning Source LLC
Chambersburg PA
CBHW030041230526
45472CB00002B/614